The Crazy Canucks

Foreword by Ken Read — Photographs by Chris Speedie

Vorwort von Ken Read — Fotografien von Chris Speedie

Avant-propos de Ken Read / Photographies par Chris Speedie

A Reidmore Book

The Crazy Canucks

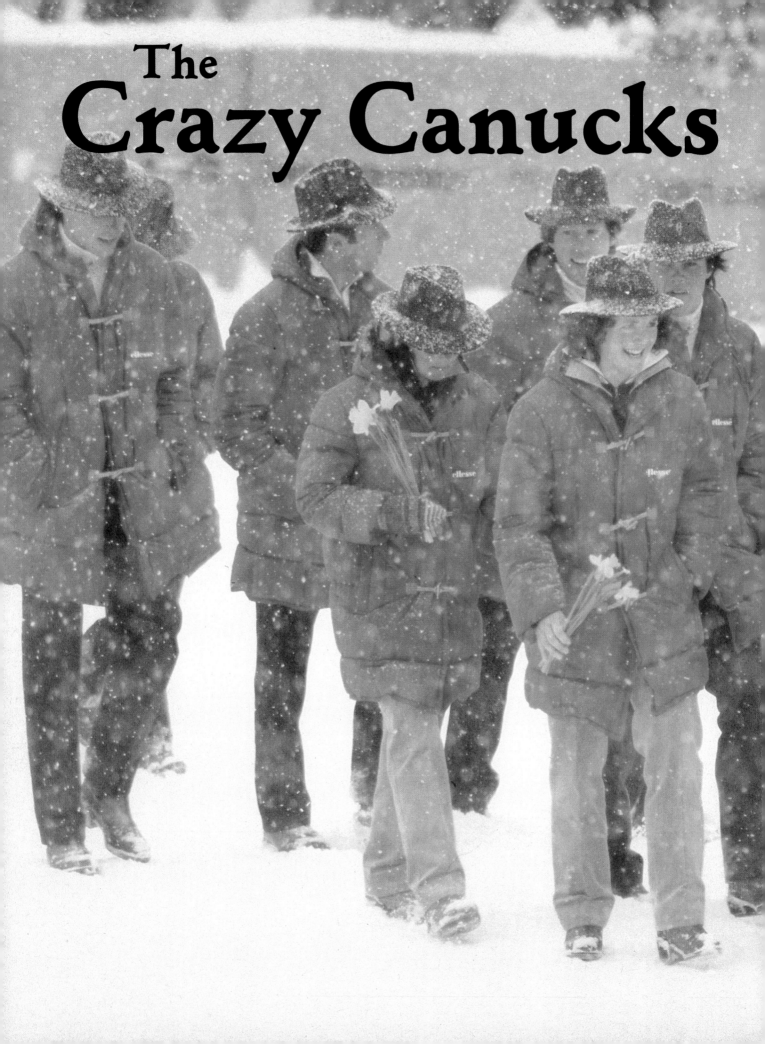

A Reidmore Book
9115 - 39 Avenue
Edmonton, Alberta, Canada T6E 5Y2

Canadian Cataloguing in Publication Data
The Crazy Canucks

ISBN 0-919091-21-0
1. Canadian National Ski Team — Pictorial Works
GV854.8C2C7 796.93'0971 C82-091257-3

Production by Van Campenhout Productions.
Separations by Color Graphics
Design and calligraphy by Ranni Pilescu
Typesetting Résistance Typographers

FOREWORD

Skiing is fun.

Skiing competitively, at the elite level, is something more than that, however. Much more.

It is work. Prodigious amounts of incredibly hard work. Weeks and months and years of weight-lifting and gymnastics, thousands of miles of running and cycling; it is pushing yourself beyond the Wall, in training, time after time after time.

It is demanding. To ski with the best in the world demands both dedication and sacrifice. Schooling and social life suffer. A single-minded sense of purpose, an overwhelming desire to be as good as you can be — to push yourself to be best — is essential.

It is challenging. It is an exercise in limit-setting and limit-smashing. Of pushing beyond the apparently possible into physical and mental territory unexplored.

Skiing competitively also teaches dependence. Without overstating the point, members of the Canadian team recognize that we all need one another. From coaches, trainers, masseurs, and servicemen, to the skiiers themselves, we all rely on one another. We help and support one another. In a sport well known for its individualism, we are truly a *team*.

A team now to be reckoned with as one of the best in the world.

In the end, for us, all the work and sacrifice has been worth it. I hope that, in these pages, a bit of the colour and excitement — the results of all that work and sacrifice — will shine through. Enjoy ''The Crazy Canucks'' — and good skiing!

Ken Read

AVANT-PROPOS

Skier, c'est amusant.

Or, pratiquer le ski de compétition, c'est beaucoup plus que ça.

Ça demande un travail acharné, des semaines, des mois et même des années d'entraînement en haltérophilie et en gymnastique, des milles de course et encore d'autres de bicyclette: le ski de compétition demande que l'on se dépasse continuellement.

Se mesurer aux meilleurs skieurs du monde exige beaucoup de bonne volonté et de grands sacrifices. Les études et la vie sociale en souffrent puisque l'unique chose qui compte, ce que l'on désire par-dessus tout, c'est de toujours s'améliorer au maximum.

Le ski de compétition est aussi un défi. C'est un sport où des objectifs sont établis, atteints et souvent même dépassés, où l'on se surpasse mentalement et physiquement pour atteindre des limites impossibles.

Aussi, le ski de compétition exige une dépendance. Jusqu'à un certain point, les membres de l'équipe canadienne ont besoin les uns des autres. Les entraîneurs, les soigneurs, les masseurs, les responsables de services et même les skieurs, tous dépendent les uns des autres. Chacun offre aux autres son appui et son aide. Le ski de compétition est reconnu comme un sport d'individualistes: pourtant, nous formons une seule et même équipe.

Cette équipe est maintenant prête à affronter les meilleurs du monde.

Tout compte fait, le dur travail et les sacrifices auront valu la peine. J'espère que dans les pages qui suivent, vous pourrez goûter la couleur et l'ivresse de ce sport, les fruits de tous nos efforts. Bonne lecture de ''Canucks: quelle équipe'' et bonne saison de ski!

Ken Read

VORWORT

Ski laufen macht Spass.

Aber Ski laufen als Wettbewerb, auf der Spitzenebene, ist mehr als das, viel mehr sogar.

Es bedeutet Arbeit. Eine unheimliche Menge unglaublich harter Arbeit. Wochen-, monate- und jahrelanges Gewichtheben und Leichtathletik treiben, Tausende von Kilometern Rennen und Rad fahren; sich Vorantreiben bis jenseits der Grenze, während des Trainings, und immer und immer wieder. Es stellt hohe Anforderungen. Um mit den Besten der Welt ski laufen zu können verlangt Hingabe und Aufopferung. Schule und Freizeit müssen zurückstehen. Unumstössliche Zielstrebigkeit und ein alles überwindender Wille so gut zu werden wie man nur kann — sich zum *äussersten* zu treiben — sind vonnöten.

Es ist eine Herausforderung. Sich dauernd Grenzen zu setzen und sie dann zu durchbrechen. Sich weiter voranzutreiben als es möglich scheint, in unerkundete körperliche und geistige Regionen.

Skilauf als Wettbewerbssport lehrt auch Zusammenhalt. Ganz ohne Pathos: Als Mitglieder der kanadischen Ski-Mannschaft haben wir sehr wohl erkannt dass wir alle aufeinander angewiesen sind. Von den Trainern, Masseuren und Hilfspersonal bis hin zu den Skiläufern selbst, wir verlassen uns Alle aufeinander. Wir helfen und unterstützen uns gegenseitig. In diesem besonders für seinen Individualismus bekannten Sport sind wir ein echtes *Team*.

Noch dazu ein Team, das zu den besten in der Welt gezählt werden muss!

Für uns hat sich all die Arbeit und das Opfer letzten Endes doch gelohnt.

Ich hoffe, dass in den folgenden Seiten etwas von der Farbe und der Aufregung — das Ergeonis all der Arbeit und Entsagung — zum Vorschein kommt. Mögen Ihnen die ''Verrückten Kanadier'' gut gefallen — und damit: ''Ski Heil''!

Ken Read

The World Cup circuit.
A stunning combination
of serenity, beauty...

... color, spectacle, and ...

speel !

Steve Podborski and
Ken Read study a slope

Ken Read

Steve Podborski, Val D'Isere

Val Gardena

Class on the sidelines

Dee Dee Haight

Video taping racers for late-night viewing

Dianne Lehodey

Todd Brooker

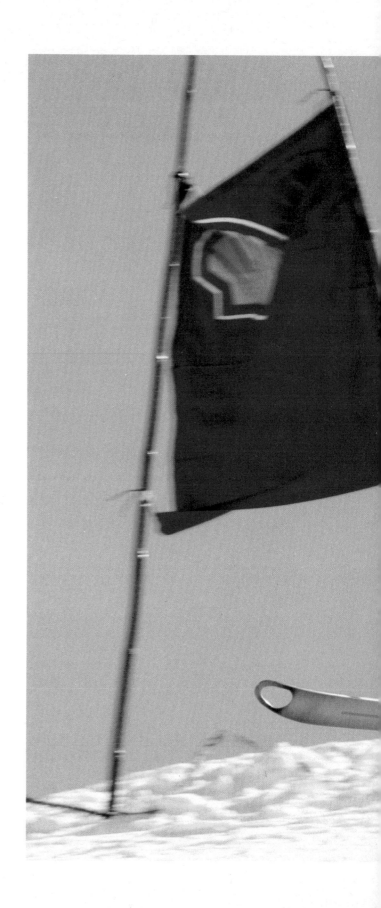

Robin McLeish

Kitzbuhel. The course in
morning

World Cup skiing is one
of Europe's most popular
spectator sports

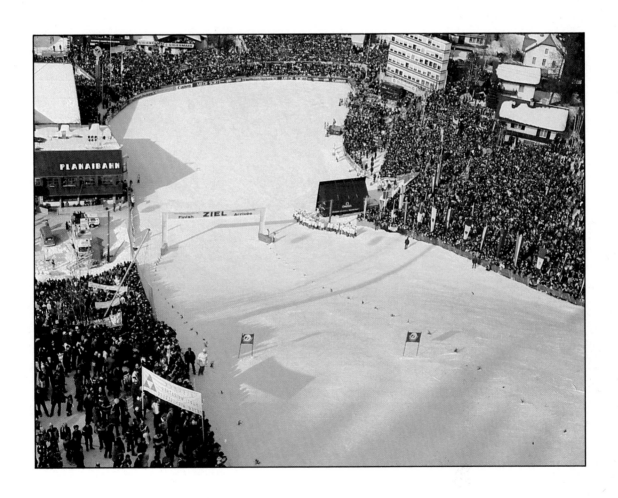

Schladming. The finish

Todd Brooker loosens up

Steve Podborski points to
another win

Steve Podborski, thrice

Three of the finest down-
hill racers in history:
Franz Klammer, Ken Read,
and Steve Podborski

Breaking bread on the road

The midnight train to Wengen

Val Gardena

Garmisch - Partenkirchen

Wengen and the Eiger

Steve Podborski. Fame

Ken Read

Robin McLeish

Chris Kent

Gary Athans

Brian O'Rourke

Doug Kerr

Gerry Sorensen

Gerry Sorensen, world champion

Waiting. Wengen

Canucks at the top of the course, Val D'Isere

Bob Styan

Fans, Schladming

Fans, Kitzbühel

The romance of skiing...
Ken Read prepares to
drive to work

Ken Read, twice

It never ends. Chris Kent on a midnight ramble

Millimeters matter. A
ski serviceman at work

Val D' Isere

Liisa Savijarvi

Opening ceremonies, Kitzbühel

Electronic homework

Todd Brooker

Steve Podborski

World champion Steve Podborski, and friends

Laurie Graham, celebrating

Steve Podborski : to success!

Todd Brooker acknowledges
the crowd after an
impressive World Cup
victory in Aspen

Todd Brooker

Laurie Graham, on her way
to a win at Mont Tremblant

Laurie Graham accepts
the crowds' congratulations
at Mont Tremblant —
her first World Cup victory,
a promise of things to
come!

... speaking of
promise — young
Andrea Bedard

New faces and old at Lake Louise.
They all have at least one thing in
common — the distinctive racing suits
of "The Crazy Canucks" — the most
exciting ski team in the world!

Thanks to:
Jacques Van Campenhout, Ed Stachoriac
Color Graphics, Husky Oil Marketing
Limited (for the photo on page 101),
Lynn Ball of the Ottawa Citizen (for
the photos on pages 99 + 100), Ken
Read for his foreword, and most
of all to Chris Speedie for his
amazing photography!

Design: R. G. Morse